The Many Animals That Live on a Farm

Children's Agriculture Books

BABY PROFESSOR
EDUCATION KIDS

Speedy Publishing LLC

40 E. Main St. #1156

Newark, DE 19711

www.speedypublishing.com

Copyright 2016

Many years ago, when people had not settled in villages and towns, they relied on getting their meat from hunting animals.

But as they developed settlements and stayed in one place for most of the year, they started to do farming and raise their own animals so that they could have a continuous supply of food without the risks and uncertainty of hunting.

This gave rise to what we call animal husbandry. People raise different animals for different purposes such as pets as companions, animals for sources of meat, milk and other benefits and other animals for transportation such as horses.

Farm animals can be categorized according to their purpose into transportation animals, meat producing animals, poultry animals, dairy animals, and animals like sheep and alpacas who are raised for their wool, fur, or feathers. Cows, buffalo, goats, and the like are dairy animals.

Chickens, turkeys, ducks, and the like are poultry. Because of their tasty meat products and various health benefits, poultry are always high in demand.

Some farm animals are used for transportation like horses, donkeys, yaks, and llamas. Aside from this, there are farm animals that are raised to be companions like dogs and cats.

BELOW IS A LIST OF FARM ANIMALS AND THEIR USE.

Alpaca - are raised for milk, transportation, fiber, meat

Buffalo - Provide meat and milk, and pull plows and wagons.

Banteng -are for meat, milk, and as work animals

Cows - are common sources of meat, milk, leather, and manure for fertilization of the soil, and as work animals

Cats - help protect the farm by eating mice; some people eat meat of cats; others treat them as pets

Chickens - are raised to provide meat, eggs and feathers

Common Carp -are for meat

Camels - are used for transportation and as sources of meat, dairy, leather

Donkeys - are used for transportation, as work animals, and for their meat in some places

Dogs - are for hunting, shepherding, herding, companionship; some cultures eat dog meat

Ducks- are raised for their eggs and meat

Emu - are for meat and feathers

Goats - provide us with milk and meat

Gayal - give us meat

Guinea pigs - are raised for meat or as pets

Geese - provide us with feathers, meat, and eggs; in some cultures geese are guard animals

Horses - are used as means of transportation

Honey Bees - are sources of honey and wax and to help in pollination

Llamas - are used for transportation, guarding herds of sheep, and for meat

Pigs - are raised for their meat and leather; other treat them as pets

Pigeons - are for meat

Rhea - are for meat, eggs, and oil

Rabbit -are raised for their meat and fur

Sheep - provide us with wool, meat, milk, leather, and vellum

Silkworm - is the source of silk

Turkeys - give us feathers and meat

Yaks - give us milk, meat, and wool, and carry loads and even people

Zebu - are raised for their meat, milk, leather, and their manure for soil fertilization, and as work animals

Aside from the animals in the list above, there are now what we call hybrid farm animals. Domesticated animals have many breeds. For example, there are over 800 breeds of cattle.

All of the breeds are used for the same purpose. However, there are some genetic differences that may be due to the environmental factors or some other factors.

BELOW IS A LIST OF HYBRID FARM ANIMALS.

Beefalo - cross breed of American bison and a domestic cow

Botswana -combination of sheep and goat

Black Rock – is a combination of Rhode Island Red and Barred Plymouth Rock chickens

Mule - is the result of a female horse and a male donkey

Yakow or Dzo - cross breed of domestic cow or bull and a yak

Yakalo - a mix of yak and buffalo

Żubroń - a combination of cattle and bison

What animals would you have on your farm, if you were a farmer?

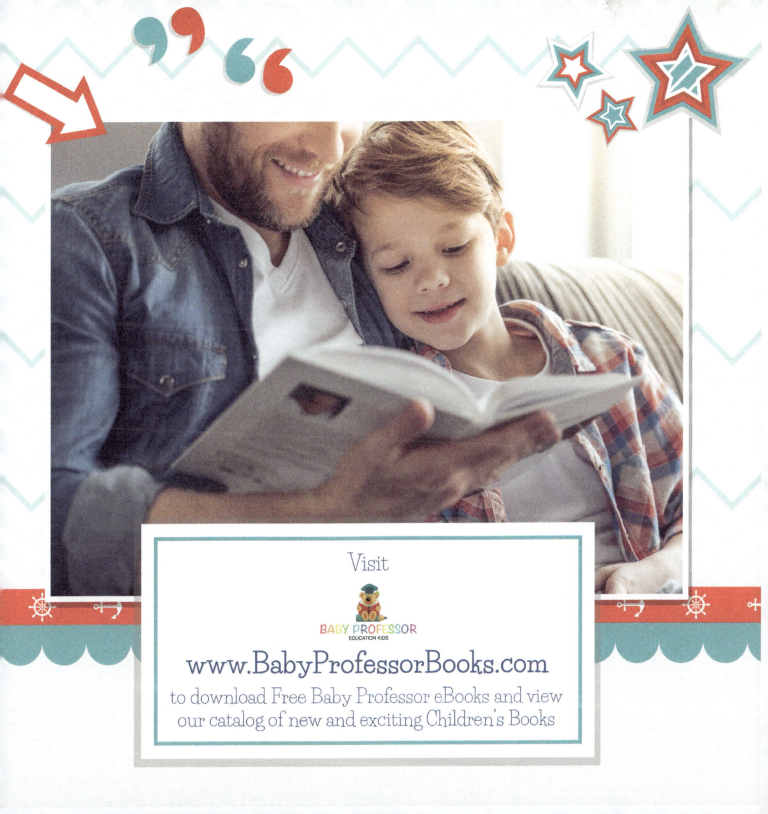

Visit

www.BabyProfessorBooks.com

to download Free Baby Professor eBooks and view
our catalog of new and exciting Children's Books

Lightning Source UK Ltd.
Milton Keynes UK
UKOW07f0612291017
311819UK00010B/206/P.